Pebble® Plus

DINOSAURS

TYRANNOSAURUS REX

A 4D Book

by Tammy Gagne

PEBBLE
a capstone imprint

Download the Capstone **4D** app!

- Ask an adult to download the Capstone 4D app.

- Scan the cover and stars inside the book for additional content.

When you scan a spread, you'll find fun extra stuff to go with this book! You can also find these things on the web at www.capstone4D.com using the password: trex.95483

Pebble Plus is published by Pebble,
1710 Roe Crest Drive, North Mankato, Minnesota 56003
www.mycapstone.com

Library of Congress Cataloging-in-Publication Data
Names: Gagne, Tammy, author.
Title: Tyrannosaurus rex : a 4D book / by Tammy Gagne.
Description: North Mankato, Minnesota : Pebble, [2019] | Series: Pebble plus. Dinosaurs | Audience: Ages 4–8.
Identifiers: LCCN 2018003056 (print) | LCCN 2018007152 (ebook) | ISBN 9781515795605 (eBook PDF) | ISBN 9781515795483 (hardcover) | ISBN 9781515795544 (pbk.)
Subjects: LCSH: Tyrannosaurus rex—Juvenile literature. | Dinosaurs—Juvenile literature.
Classification: LCC QE862.S3 (ebook) | LCC QE862.S3 G338 2018 (print) | DDC 567.912/9—dc23
LC record available at https://lccn.loc.gov/2018003056

Editorial Credits
Hank Musolf, editor; Charmaine Whitman, designer;
Kelly Garvin, media researcher; Laura Manthe, production specialist;
Illustrator, Capstone Press/Jon Hughes

Design Elements
Shutterstock/Krasovski Dmitri

Printed and bound in China.
000309

Note to Parents and Teachers

The Dinosaurs set supports national science standards related to life science. This book describes and illustrates tyrannosaurus rex. The images support early readers in understanding the text. The repetition of words and phrases helps early readers learn new words. This book also introduces early readers to subject-specific vocabulary words, which are defined in the Glossary section. Early readers may need assistance to read some words and to use the Table of Contents, Glossary, Read More, Internet Sites, Critical Thinking Questions, and Index sections of the book.

Table of Contents

Meet the Tyrannosaurus Rex

Tyrannosaurus rex was a dinosaur that ate meat. It hunted many other dinosaur species.

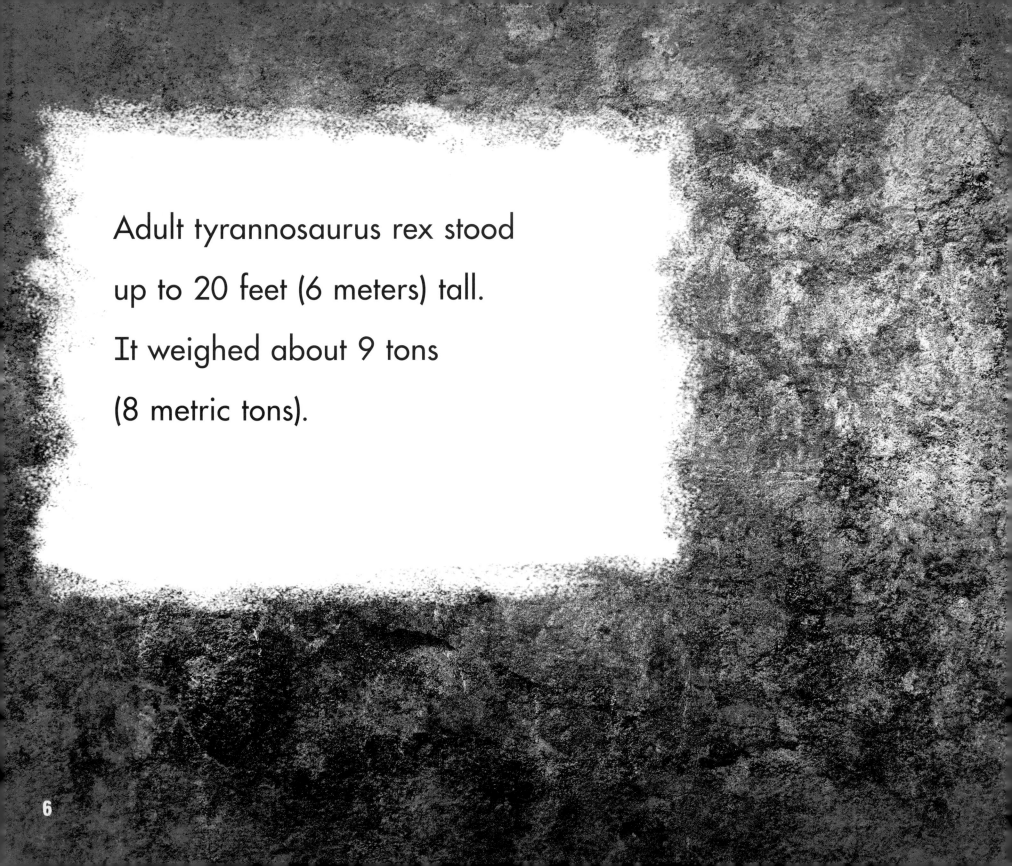

Adult tyrannosaurus rex stood
up to 20 feet (6 meters) tall.
It weighed about 9 tons
(8 metric tons).

Tyrannosaurus rex had a large head and tail. Its strong back legs helped it run up to 25 miles (40 kilometers) per hour. But its short front legs could not reach its mouth.

Bone Crushers

Tyrannosaurus rex was a carnivore. It hunted other dinosaurs. It could eat 500 pounds (230 kilograms) of meat in one bite!

Tyrannosaurus rex teeth were cone shaped. The teeth could grab and bite prey. Strong jaws crushed bones.

What Big Feet They Had

Tyrannosaurus rex lived about 70 million years ago. It lived in western North America. Scientists think tyrannosaurus rex moved to different places.

Scientists found tyrannosaurus rex bones in Montana.

A tyrannosaurus rex footprint was found in New Mexico. It was 34 inches (86 centimeters) long!

Working Together

Tyrannosaurus rex

was a smart species.

It had a large brain.

Scientists think this species hunted in packs. The fast, young dinosaurs chased prey. The slower adults killed it when they caught up.

Glossary

carnivore—an animal that eats meat

prey—an animal that is hunted by another animal

scientist—a person who studies the workings of the world

species—a group of animals who share numerous traits

Read More

Nunn, Daniel. *Tyrannosaurus Rex*. All About Dinosaurs. Chicago: Capstone Heinemann Library, 2015.

Stewart, Melissa. *Why Did T. rex Have Short Arms?: And Other Questions About Dinosaurs.* Good Question! New York: Sterling Children's Books, 2014.

Wegwerth, A.L. *Tyrannosaurus Rex*. Little Paleontologist. North Mankato, MN: Capstone Press, 2015.

Internet Sites

Use FactHound to find Internet sites related to this book.

Visit www.facthound.com

Just type in 9781515795483 and go.

Check out projects, games and lots more at
www.capstonekids.com

Critical Thinking Questions

1. How did tyrannosaurus rex feed itself if its front legs couldn't reach its mouth?

2. How do you think the shape of the tyrannosaurus rex's teeth helped it in hunting?

3. How might scientists learn from fossils that tyrannosaurus rex lived in groups?

Index